SAN FRANCISCO

by Marty Gitlin

Published by ABDO Publishing Company, 8000 West 78th Street, Edina, Minnesota 55439. Copyright © 2011 by Abdo Consulting Group, Inc. International copyrights reserved in all countries. No part of this book may be reproduced in any form without written permission from the publisher. SportsZone™ is a trademark and logo of ABDO Publishing Company.

Printed in the United States of America,
North Mankato, Minnesota
112010
012011

Editor: Chrös McDougall
Copy Editor: Nicholas Cafarelli
Interior Design and Production: Carol Castro
Cover Design: Craig Hinton

Photo Credits: Marcio Jose Sanchez/AP Images, cover; AP Images, 1, 12, 15, 16, 19, 20, 23, 25, 26, 31, 33, 42 (middle and bottom), 43 (top); Kyodo via AP Images, 4, 43 (bottom); Tony Gutierrez/AP Images, 7, 9; Library of Congress, 10, 42 (top); Focus on Sports/Getty Images, 28; Eric Riseberg/AP Images, 34, 43 (middle), 47; Paul Sakuma/AP Images, 37; Kristy MacDonald/AP Images, 38; Ben Margot/AP Images, 41; Justin Sullivan/AP Images, 44

Library of Congress Cataloging-in-Publication Data
Gitlin, Marty.
  San Francisco Giants / Marty Gitlin.
      p. cm. — (Inside MLB)
  Includes index.
  ISBN 978-1-61714-058-7
  1. San Francisco Giants (Baseball team)—History—Juvenile literature. I. Title.
  GV875.S34.G57 2011
  796.357'640979461—dc22
                              2010038745

TABLE OF CONTENTS

CHAPTER 1

A GIANT CHAMPIONSHIP

Edgar Renteria stepped to the plate with two men on, two outs, and no score in the seventh inning of the fifth game of the 2010 World Series. Texas Rangers ace Cliff Lee had a decision to make: Pitch to Renteria, or walk him?

It was a tough decision. Renteria had been red-hot in the playoffs. Meanwhile, on-deck hitter Aaron Rowand was ice-cold. First base was open. And Lee had already fallen behind in the count by throwing two balls outside the strike zone to Renteria.

But Lee was not only a gutsy pitcher, he was also one of the best in baseball. He was confident he could get anybody out. So he tried to sneak a fastball past Renteria. And Renteria blasted it high and just over the left-field fence.

Giants 3, Rangers 0.

Giants shortstop Edgar Renteria rounds third after hitting a three-run homer in Game 5 of the 2010 World Series. He was named the Series' Most Valuable Player.

The game was not over, but it just as well might have been. The Giants' pitchers had been dominant during the play-offs. Ace Tim Lincecum gave up one run through eight innings in Game 5. Then closer Brian Wilson shut out Texas in the ninth to secure the 3–1 victory.

When Rangers outfielder Nelson Cruz swung and missed at the last pitch, the Giants had won their first World Series title since 1954. More importantly, it was their first title since moving to San Francisco in 1958. "San Francisco is going nuts," Wilson said. "We're going nuts and it feels really good."

The 2010 season was not always so promising for the Giants. After several medio-cre seasons, the Giants had a mediocre start to the season. They were 41–40 and fourth in the National League (NL) West Division halfway through the season. But then the team's talented young pitching staff blossomed.

The Giants won nine of their next 10 games and 21 of 26 to pull into second place behind the San Diego Padres. They finally caught the Padres on September 10. The teams battled for the division title and wild card playoff spot the rest of the way.

It all came down to the final series between the two

Fear the Beard

Several Giants players grew beards during their run to the 2010 World Series title. Among them was closer Brian Wilson. He sported a thick black beard by the end of the season. Wilson's beard became so popular that fans started a "Fear the Beard" campaign and began showing up at the ballpark wearing fake black beards. Wilson was more popular for his talent, though. He led all of baseball with 48 saves in 2010 and added six more in the postseason.

Aubrey Huff, *top left*, Brian Wilson, *bottom left*, and Buster Posey celebrate after getting the final out of the 2010 World Series.

teams. The Giants appeared to be doomed when they lost the first two of three games. But talented young pitcher Jonathan Sanchez and five relievers combined to give the Giants a 3–0 shutout in the final game of the season. The Giants were heading to the playoffs.

Sanchez combined with Lincecum, Matt Cain, and rookie Madison Bumgarner to form a dominant pitching staff. The Giants led the NL in earned-run average (ERA) and set a franchise record with 1,331 strikeouts. Meanwhile, Wilson led the NL with 48 saves.

BEST IN BASEBALL?

Tim Lincecum is only 5 feet, 11 inches and a skinny 170 pounds. His long, stringy dark hair waves in the breeze as he walks. But the man nicknamed "The Freak" is arguably the greatest pitcher in the game.

Lincecum throws a 95-miles-per-hour fastball, which is unusually fast for a pitcher his size. He also tosses a baffling change-up that often has hitters waving at nothing but air. And his best pitch is a curveball that drops a foot as it approaches the plate.

It's no wonder he owned a sparkling 56–27 career record through 2010 and led the NL in strikeouts three straight years. Most pitchers yield more than a hit per inning, but through 2010, Lincecum has pitched 811 innings in his career and given up just 666 hits. He is also one of just a few pitchers to average more than one strikeout per inning.

However, the Giants struggled at the plate. Catcher Buster Posey, who was the 2010 NL Rookie of the Year, was the only hitter to bat over .300. Only shortstop Juan Uribe and first baseman Aubrey Huff had more than 67 runs batted in (RBIs). The Giants also lacked speed. They finished tied for last in the NL in stolen bases. Many believed the Giants' weak hitting would hold them back from winning the World Series title.

It did not stop them in the NL Division Series (NLDS). The Giants' pitchers gave up just nine runs in a four-game win over the Atlanta Braves. The Giants were considered big underdogs against the two-time defending NL champion Philadelphia Phillies in the NL Championship Series (NLCS). The Phillies had great pitching and batting.

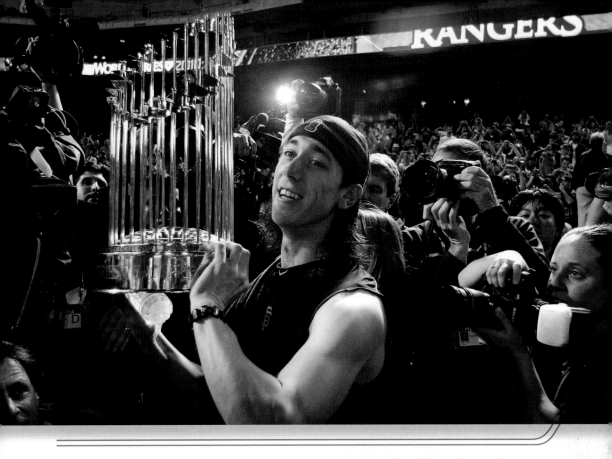

Tim Lincecum carries the World Series trophy after the Giants beat the Rangers in 2010. He went 4–1 in the postseason with a 2.43 ERA.

The Giants were unfazed. They split the first two games in Philadelphia. Then they won two of three in San Francisco. They trailed 2–0 in Game 6, but fought back to tie it at 2–2. Uribe then slammed a home run in the eighth inning to give the Giants a 3–2 lead. When Wilson closed out the ninth inning, the Giants had won their first NL pennant since 2002.

When the Giants beat the Rangers in the World Series, they were the best team in all of Major League Baseball (MLB). It was their first title since moving to San Francisco, but it was just another chapter in the team's storied history.

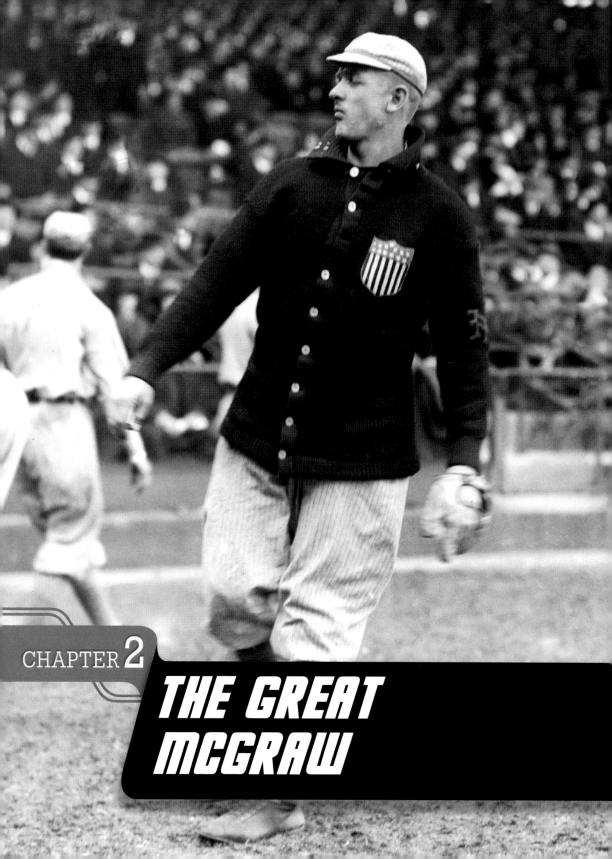

CHAPTER 2

THE GREAT McGRAW

John B. Day and Jim Mutrie founded the team that became the Giants in 1883. They also owned the New York Metropolitans of the American Association. They named their new team the Gothams and placed them into the NL, where they have remained ever since.

Mutrie managed the club in its early seasons. He immediately established a winning tradition. His teams won the NL pennant in both 1888 and 1889. Pitchers Tim Keefe and Mickey Welch led the way. They combined for 116 victories

Name That Team

The Giants' name actually came upon the team by accident. After an impressive extra-inning win over the Philadelphia Quakers on June 3, 1885, ecstatic manager Jim Mutrie blurted out that his team played like giants. The name stuck.

Christy Mathewson won 373 games during his 17-year career from 1900 to 1916. All but one victory was with the Giants.

Giants manager John McGraw, *right*, meets with St. Louis Cardinals manager Gabby Street prior to Game 3 of the 1931 World Series.

Skipping the Series

The AL was created in 1901. The first World Series, between the NL and the AL, was played in 1903. However, there was no World Series played in 1904. That was because Giants manager John McGraw and owner John Brush considered the AL to be inferior. The Giants won the NL pennant that year with a franchise best 106–47 record.

in those two years after winning 76 between them in 1885.

A new pitching duo emerged in 1894. Jouett Meekin and Amos Rusie combined for 69 wins that season. Then they led the team—by then known as the Giants—to an 1894 playoff sweep of the Baltimore Orioles. But the team was not able to find a manager who would stick, which brought inconsistency to the team. Then, during the 1902 season, the team hired an arrogant and combative infielder named John McGraw to be a player/manager.

McGraw was considered one of the most dominant figures in the sport for several reasons. He was accused of cheating. He battled with umpires and baseball officials. And he often displayed a violent temper on the field and in addressing his team.

But the man nicknamed "Little Napoleon" knew how to win. And so did Giants pitcher Christy Mathewson. The young right-hander was just beginning to blossom when McGraw became manager. Mathewson won 33 games in 1904. He led the league with 31 the following year as the Giants exceeded 100 victories. The team won the NL pennant both seasons.

In the 1905 World Series, Mathewson threw three shutout victories over the Philadelphia Athletics. His 2–0 blanking of the Athletics in Game 5 secured the championship. Mathewson received plenty of help that season. Fellow pitchers Red Ames and Joe "Iron Man" McGinnity combined for 43 wins.

McGraw and Mathewson continued to make the Giants one of the best teams in baseball. They stayed together from 1903 until 1916. The Giants only had one losing season during that time. They won 100 or more games in four different seasons. However, the Giants struggled to win titles. They lost in the World Series in 1911, 1912, 1913, and 1917.

Their fortunes changed in 1921. Mathewson had long since retired. But the Giants now boasted the highest-scoring offense in the NL. First baseman George "High Pockets" Kelly, third baseman Frankie Frisch, and outfielder Ross

A TRUE ACE

Christy Mathewson was among the most consistent and talented pitchers in baseball history. He spent nearly his entire career with the Giants and won between 22 and 30 games every season from 1903 to 1914. He also led the NL five times in strikeouts and ERA. His highest ERA of those five was 2.06. His 1.14 ERA in 1909 was the best in major league history until St. Louis Cardinals right-hander Bob Gibson posted a 1.12 ERA in 1968.

But Mathewson also impressed those who knew him as a person. His demeanor was quite the opposite of that of his manager, John McGraw. "He handed the game a certain touch of class, an indefinable lift in culture, brains, and personality," wrote sportswriter Grantland Rice.

Mathewson's total of 373 career victories is tied for third all-time behind Cy Young (511) and Walter Johnson (417).

Youngs all had more than 100 RBIs. Seven of the eight regular players batted .299 or better.

The Giants met the New York Yankees in the World Series. The Yankees won the first two games and three of the first five. It appeared that the 1921 Giants were about to suffer the same fate as they had in the past four World Series appearances. But the Giants won the last three games. Pitcher Art Nehf threw a 1–0 shutout in Game 8 to give the Giants their first championship in 16 years. Then they repeated the feat in 1922. This time they swept past the Yankees 4–0.

The 1922 Giants featured a pitching staff that was far less talented than those of previous Giants teams. McGraw received the credit for getting the most out of those pitchers.

Hall of Famer George "High Pockets" Kelly played first base for the Giants and helped the team win the World Series in 1921 and 1922.

"One ought to say that John McGraw's Giants won the title, rather than merely the Giants," exclaimed one *New York Times* article after the 1922 season.

The Giants continued to cruise after their 1922 World Series victory. They won their third consecutive NL pennant in 1923 and their fourth in 1924. But the Giants lost in the World Series both years. During McGraw's 31 years in charge, the Giants only had three losing seasons. One of them was in 1932. McGraw retired during that season.

Slugging player/manager Bill Terry replaced McGraw. He quickly returned the Giants to their winning ways.

CHAPTER 3

TERRY, OTT, AND THE SHOT

T he Giants featured a number of good hitters into the early 1920s. But aside from George "High Pockets" Kelly, none struck fear in the hearts of opposing pitchers. That certainly changed later in the decade. By that time, the Giants had acquired two of the best sluggers in the history of the sport. And, as it turns out, one would follow the other as the team's manager.

The first to arrive was first baseman Bill Terry. He exceeded 100 RBIs every year from 1927 to 1932. He led the league with 254 hits and a .401 batting average in 1930. Outfielder Mel Ott established himself as a full-time player in 1928. He maintained his greatness for far longer than Terry. Ott drove in 100 or more runs in eight consecutive seasons. He also led the NL in home runs six times during his 22 seasons.

Mel Ott drove in 100 or more runs in eight consecutive seasons from 1929 to 1936. He played for the Giants from 1926 to 1947.

In June 1932, Terry took over as player/manager. After the Giants' rare losing season in 1932, they came back to win the NL pennant in Terry's first full season. Ott performed well during that 1933 season. But the true star was a left-handed pitcher named Carl Hubbell. His specialty was the screwball. He had enjoyed several strong seasons. But in 1933, Hubbell was just reaching his prime. He won 23 games, led the league with a 1.66 ERA, and was named Most Valuable Player (MVP). It was the first of five straight 20-win seasons for the future Hall of Famer.

The Giants faced the Washington Senators in the World Series. Several heroes emerged for New York as the Giants beat the Senators in five games. Hubbell did not allow an earned run in two victories. Fellow pitcher Hal Schumacher allowed just one run in winning Game 2. Ott, meanwhile, hit a game-winning home run in the 10th inning to win Game 5—and the Series. An estimated 2,000 joyous fans greeted the Giants at the bus terminal when the team returned from Washington DC.

The defeat of the heavily favored Senators was a surprise. But so was the trip to the World Series. Even Giants fans had lower expectations after the team's losing record in 1932.

Mowing Them Down

The 1934 All-Star Game was at the Giants' home field, the Polo Grounds. Giants' pitcher Carl Hubbell put on a legendary All-Star Game performance for his home crowd. Hubbell struck out five consecutive Hall of Famers with his screwball, which darts the opposite way of a curveball. He fanned Babe Ruth, Lou Gehrig, and Jimmie Foxx to end the first inning. Then he struck out Al Simmons and Joe Cronin to start the second.

Bill Terry, *right*, and Mel Ott were two of the great Giants players of the 1920s and 1930s. Both later became managers of the team.

"Thus the team which had begun the [season] carrying with it little more than the best wishes of its friends that it would make a reasonably fair run at [contention], now is in possession of the baseball championship of the world," wrote the *New York Times* the next day.

New York was at the center of the baseball universe in 1936 and 1937. That is because the Giants played against the Yankees in the World Series after both seasons. The Yankees were baseball's elite team at the time. They featured some of baseball's all-time greats, such as Lou Gehrig and Joe

Carl Hubbell used a screwball pitch to help him post five consecutive 20-win seasons from 1933 to 1937. He was the NL MVP in 1933 and 1936.

DiMaggio. Ott, Hubbell, and the Giants could not match the Yankees during those World Series. Hubbell won Game 1 of the 1936 Fall Classic, but the Yankees won four of the last five to take the title. The Giants won just one World Series game the next year.

The Giants had been a very successful team so far in their history. After 1937 they had won 14 NL pennants and four World Series. But they soon slipped into mediocrity. Terry retired as a player after the 1936 season. An aging Ott could no longer carry the offense, which by then included several weak hitters. The Giants had some decent pitchers, but none that could be considered an ace such as Hubbell in his prime. The Giants had a strong 85–67 season when Ott took over as manager in 1942. But they stumbled badly during World War II, as some of their players went off to fight overseas.

Included among those lost to the war effort was power-hitting first baseman Johnny Mize. He batted .305 with 110 RBIs for the Giants in 1942, then served in the Navy for the next three years. He returned to lead the NL with 137 runs, 51 home runs, and 138 RBIs in 1947. He also hit 40 home runs the next season.

Giants fans were stunned when Leo Durocher was hired as manager in 1948. After all, Durocher had been managing the hated Brooklyn Dodgers.

But those same fans quickly warmed to Durocher when he transformed the team from also-rans to contenders.

In 1951, the Giants had a mediocre 59–51 start to the season. Then they got hot. They went on a 16-game winning streak. The Giants finished the season on a 39–8 run to tie the Dodgers for the NL pennant. That meant they had to play a three-game playoff to determine the champion.

Integration

Two years after Jackie Robinson broke the color barrier in the major leagues, the Giants signed two African-American players of their own. One of them was Monte Irvin. He had been denied the opportunity to play until he was past 30 years old. Irvin emerged as a top-flight outfielder. In the team's pennant year of 1951, he batted .312 and led the NL with 121 RBIs. The other was outfielder Hank Thompson, who enjoyed several strong seasons as a starter for the Giants.

The teams split the first two games. It looked bleak for the Giants in the third and deciding game. They were trailing 4–2 with one out in the ninth inning. But they also had two runners on base.

Giants third baseman Bobby Thomson stepped up to the plate. The crowd was roaring at the Polo Grounds, the Giants' home field. Dodgers relief pitcher Ralph Branca had just entered the game. Thomson gazed out at Branca. The right-hander was crouched over on the mound. He was ready to deliver one of the most important pitches in baseball history.

Thomson told himself to be patient. But Branca threw a fastball right down the middle that Thomson just stared at. Strike one. Then Branca fired another fastball. This one was high and inside. Thomson did not wait and watch this time. He took a mighty swing and smashed a line drive into the left-field stands. The Giants won, 5–4. They were NL champions. Thomson's three-run homer became forever known as "The Shot Heard 'Round the World."

Brooklyn fans stood in stunned silence. New York fans hugged each other and shouted with joy. After a 13-year absence, the Giants had won the pennant. And in the radio

Johnny on the Spot

Plenty of pressure was placed on left-hander Johnny Antonelli when the Giants acquired him in a trade with the Milwaukee Braves before the 1954 season. But Antonelli responded by becoming the team's ace pitcher. Antonelli played a key role in the Giants' run to a World Series title by compiling a 21–7 record and NL-best 2.30 ERA. He continued to perform well, winning 81 games in the next five years. He was an All-Star five times between 1954 and 1959.

Bobby Thomson is greeted by his Giants teammates at home plate after he clinched the NL pennant with "The Shot Heard 'Round the World."

booth, Giants announcer Russ Hodges made the famous call as Thomson rounded the bases: "THE GIANTS WIN THE PENNANT! THE GIANTS WIN THE PENNANT!" he screamed over and over. "AND THEY'RE GOING CRAZY!"

The Giants faced the AL champion Yankees in the World Series. The Giants carried their momentum into the Series. They won two of the first three games. But then they lost the next two by a combined score of 19–3. The Giants held close in Game 6, but outfielder Hank Bauer made a great catch on a line drive hit by Sal Yvars to clinch the title.

THE "SAY HEY" KID

Willie Mays was the 1951 NL Rookie of the Year. His offensive numbers skyrocketed after that. In 1954, he led the NL with a .345 batting average, hit 41 home runs, and won the MVP Award. He was the MVP again in 1965, when he hit a career-high 52 home runs. During his 22-year career, Mays appeared in a record 24 All-Star Games. He led the NL in home runs and stolen bases four times and triples three times. His brilliance in center field was rewarded with 12 Gold Glove Awards. He was simply great in just about every part of the game.

"He would routinely do things you never saw anyone else do," said Giants president Peter Magowan. "He'd score from first base on a single. He'd take two bases on a pop-up. He'd throw somebody out at the plate on one bounce. And the bigger the game, the better he played."

The Giants were back in the World Series three years later. The opposing Cleveland Indians were heavily favored. They had won an AL-record 111 games that season.

The teams were tied at 2–2 in the eighth inning of Game 1. The Indians had two runners on base when slugger Vic Wertz stepped to the plate. Wertz smashed a pitch deep to center field. It looked like a sure double. But the Giants' speedy center fielder Willie Mays sprinted back and snagged the ball with his back turned to home plate. Many still consider that to be the greatest catch in baseball history made by the greatest outfielder in baseball history.

Giants pinch-hitter Dusty Rhodes slammed a three-run homer in the 10th inning to give his team the win. After that, all the life seemed to be

Willie Mays added to his legend by making this incredible catch in Game 1 of the 1954 World Series.

sucked out of the Indians. The Giants swept the Series in four games. And it was Mays's amazing catch that stole the show. Years later, it is still known simply as "The Catch."

The 1954 World Series would be the last for the Giants while playing in New York. Three years later, owner Horace Stoneham announced he was moving the team to San Francisco. It was a painful time for Giants fans. But at least they had many great memories to look back on.

COMING TO CALIFORNIA

Times were changing in New York City in the 1950s, but the Giants could not keep up with the changes. The rundown Polo Grounds was scheduled for demolition. Attendance at Giants games had plummeted. Owner Horace Stoneham began searching for a new home for his team.

On August 19, 1957, Stoneham announced he had accepted an offer to move the Giants to San Francisco starting with the 1958 season. The move coincided with that of the Brooklyn Dodgers. They were set to leave New York for Los Angeles at the same time.

The Giants played their final game in New York on September 29, 1957. The mood of the fans at the Polo Grounds that day was described by *New York Times* reporter Milton Bracker.

"Under a big banner somewhat forlornly pleading, 'STAY

Orlando Cepeda helped turn the San Francisco Giants into a winning team. He was the 1958 NL Rookie of the Year.

First baseman Willie McCovey played 19 seasons with the Giants. He led the NL in home runs three times and was the 1969 NL MVP.

TEAM, STAY,' in the right field section, the mob began: 'We want Stoneham!'" Bracker wrote.

"The crowd obviously didn't 'want' him out of love; they blamed him for moving the team to the [West] Coast.

"'We want Stoneham!' they insisted. Then, as if anyone might have misunderstood, they turned it into a little song.

"'We want Stoneham; We want Stoneham—with a rope around his neck!'"

The mood was quite different in San Francisco. The Giants were welcomed to the Bay Area with a parade. And the fans supported their team.

The Giants finished near the top of the NL in attendance during the first few seasons. Their numbers only increased when the Giants moved into the new Candlestick Park in 1960.

They also had a strong team for which to root. Willie Mays remained the Giants' top player when they moved to San Francisco. Rookie first baseman Orlando Cepeda provided Mays with some much-needed help when he arrived in 1958. Cepeda was switched to the outfield when slugging first baseman Willie McCovey moved into the lineup full-time in 1960. Meanwhile, a high-kicking right-hander named Juan Marichal emerged as one of the best pitchers in the game during the early 1960s.

Those players combined to turn the Giants from an average team to a winning team. The Giants continued to improve until peaking in 1962. They had a 103–62 record and won the pennant that season under manager Alvin Dark. The Giants received a combined 109 home runs and 353 RBIs from Mays, Cepeda, and outfielder Felipe Alou. All three also batted .300 or better. Meanwhile, surprising pitcher Jack Sanford had easily his best season, posting a 24–7 record.

"Stretch"

Willie McCovey was nicknamed "Stretch" because of his lanky 6-foot-4 frame. But he was also one of the top sluggers in baseball. The left-handed hitting first baseman won NL Rookie of the Year honors in 1959 despite having just 192 at-bats. By 1963, he had emerged as one of the game's most feared hitters when he led the league with 44 home runs. McCovey blasted more than 30 homers in six straight seasons starting in 1965. He led the NL with 36 in 1968 and had a career-high 45 in 1969, when he won the MVP Award.

The Giants finished in a tie with rival Los Angeles Dodgers for the 1962 NL title. The Dodgers brought a 4–2 lead into the ninth inning of the third and deciding playoff game. But the Giants clinched a playoff victory by scoring four runs in that inning. An estimated 75,000 delirious fans greeted the Giants at the airport upon their return home. San Francisco sportscaster Bruce MacGowan recalled his feelings that day.

Juan Marichal

The greatness of NL pitchers such as Sandy Koufax and Bob Gibson stole some attention from Giants right-hander Juan Marichal. But Marichal was among the premier pitchers of any era. His distinctive high-kicking style on the mound and great curveball resulted in eight seasons of 18 wins or more, including league highs of 25 victories in 1963 and 26 in 1968. Marichal also had a 21–11 record and NL-best 2.13 ERA in 1969. He was inducted into the Hall of Fame in 1983.

"I vividly remember listening to the game as a kid in fourth grade with my buddies on the playground just after school had let out," he wrote. "We were all huddled around a little transistor radio listening to [Giants broadcaster] Lon Simmons call the final out before we jumped out and screamed like a bunch of little banshees. Longtime Bay Area residents likened the reaction of the victory that day to the [victory] celebrations of 1945, when the Japanese surrendered to end World War II."

The 1962 World Series against the Yankees was equally dramatic. The teams traded wins from the start. Sanford performed brilliantly in Game 7, but the Giants lost 1–0. The Giants held the Yankees to a .199 batting average in the Fall Classic. However, they could not score enough runs to win.

Juan Marichal, known for his high leg kick, won more games (191) than any other pitcher in the 1960s.

The Giants continued to contend in the 1960s. But they always fell just short of winning pennants. They finished within three games of first place in 1964, 1965, 1966, 1967, and 1969. Mays and McCovey continued to be good hitters.

The addition of third baseman Jim Ray Hart and outfielder Bobby Bonds provided more offense. Meanwhile, right-hander Gaylord Perry combined with Marichal to provide a great 1–2 pitching punch. The pair led a charge to the division title

GAYLORD PERRY

Pitcher Gaylord Perry broke out in 1966, posting a 21–8 record. He maintained an ERA under 3.00 for the next three years, and then led the NL with 23 victories in 1970. But the Giants wanted Cleveland left-hander Sam McDowell. So they traded Perry and shortstop Frank Duffy for McDowell after the 1971 season. McDowell had been a talented but underachieving pitcher for many years. He failed badly in San Francisco. Meanwhile, Perry won 24 games and the AL Cy Young Award in 1972 and excelled for many years.

Controversy, however, followed Perry. Many believed he placed substances on the ball that made it drop. Managers sometimes demanded that umpires visit Perry on the mound to frisk him, but they never found anything. After retirement, Perry admitted that he indeed "doctored" the ball. Some argue that since he did cheat, he should be removed from the Baseball Hall of Fame.

in 1971. But the Giants lost to the Pittsburgh Pirates in the NL Championship Series (NLCS).

The Giants were not able to build upon that 1971 season. Perry was traded to the Cleveland Indians before the 1972 season. Meanwhile, Mays, McCovey, and Marichal all slipped out of their primes. Their replacements simply did not match their talent, and the Giants faded into mediocrity.

The late 1970s and early 1980s were marked by more inconsistency. In 1981, the Giants hired Frank Robinson as the first African-American manager in the NL. Sluggers such as Jack Clark and Darrell Evans provided power. But the fans had little to cheer about when they departed.

In 1985, the Giants lost 100 games for the first time in their history. They would

Bobby Bonds had a record five seasons with at least 30 home runs and 30 stolen bases. He did it with the Giants in 1970 and 1973.

soon finish a fifteenth consecutive season without reaching the postseason in 1986. But thankfully for Giants fans, another pennant race was on the horizon.

30–30

Bobby Bonds, who played right field for the Giants from 1968 to 1974, hit 30 home runs and stole 30 bases in the same season five times, including twice with the Giants. Through 2010, Bobby's son, Barry Bonds, was the only other big-league player to have five 30–30 seasons. Barry had three of his 30–30 seasons during his 15 years with the Giants.

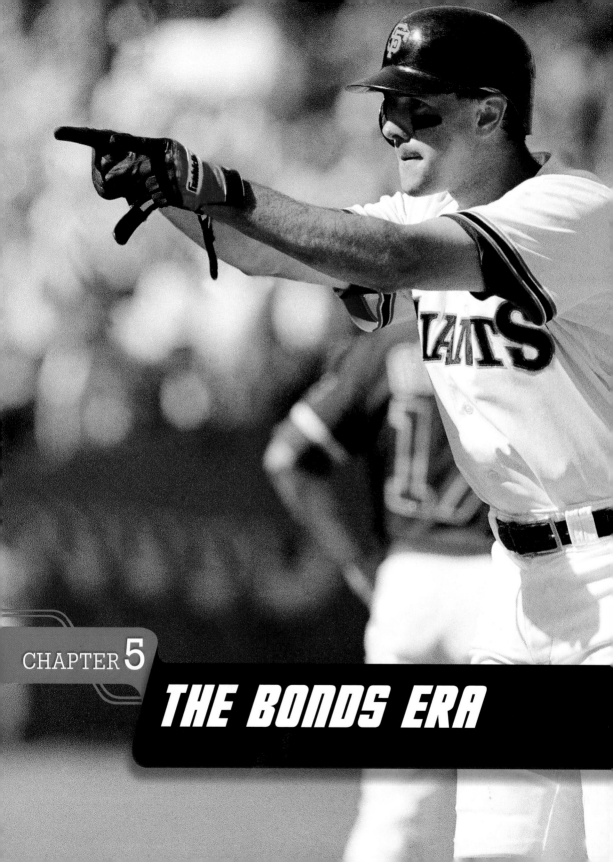

CHAPTER 5

THE BONDS ERA

I n 1986, the Giants launched the "You Gotta Like These Kids" campaign. They hoped it would get fans excited about the team's talented young players. Two of the players were first baseman Will Clark and second baseman Robby Thompson. The Giants figured to build around those two for years to come.

The trumpeting of the new Giants was indeed warranted. The team had lost a franchise-record 100 games in 1985. But then they won 83 games in 1986 in manager Roger Craig's first full season. He then continued to transform the Giants into regular contenders.

Will Clark

Will Clark was a line-drive hitter who regularly batted over .300, but he also boasted good power. He averaged 24 home runs and 95 RBIs in seven full seasons with the team. He led the NL with 109 RBIs and 100 walks in 1988 and finished second in the MVP voting a year later when he batted .333 with 111 RBIs.

Will Clark helped the Giants overcome the Chicago Cubs in the 1989 NLCS. The Giants advanced to their first World Series since 1962.

Clark blossomed in 1987. He batted .308 with 35 home runs to lead a surge to the 1987 division title. The Giants were one victory from the pennant. However, the St. Louis Cardinals shut out the Giants in the last two games of the NLCS.

The Giants returned to the playoffs in 1989 behind Clark and slugging outfielder Kevin Mitchell. The latter hit 47 home runs that season. The Giants then won the last three games of the NLCS to defeat the Chicago Cubs. That led to their first World Series berth since 1962. Clark was the hero in the win over the Cubs. He hit .650 with two home runs and eight RBIs.

The World Series was not memorable for the Giants' play on the field. The neighboring Oakland Athletics swept the Giants in the World Series. But the Series is remembered for an earthquake that struck the Bay Area before Game 3. The Giants and Athletics played only miles away from each other on the coast of the San Francisco Bay. After a 10-day delay, the World Series resumed and the A's completed the sweep.

The Giants had another winning season in 1990. But they dropped to below .500 in each of the following two years.

Loma Prieta Earthquake

Baseball fever hit the San Francisco Bay area when the Giants and Athletics won their pennants and met in the 1989 World Series. But the games soon faded into the background when an earthquake devastated the area. The teams were preparing for Game 3 at Candlestick Park on October 17, 1989, when the entire stadium shook. No one inside the stadium was seriously hurt. However, the earthquake left 63 people dead, thousands more injured, and caused billons of dollars in damage in the Bay Area.

An earthquake struck the Bay Area, forcing a 10-day delay of the 1989 World Series. These fans returned to Candlestick Park wearing hard hats.

The team hired Dusty Baker as manager in 1993. That same season, they signed free agent outfielder Barry Bonds. The son of former Giants star Bobby Bonds had blossomed into a top slugger while with the Pittsburgh Pirates. Both moves proved to be good ones.

The Giants won 103 games in 1993 with Baker as manager as Bonds earned the NL MVP Award. He had an NL-best 46 home runs and 123 RBIs. However, the Giants fell short of the playoffs.

The Giants won another division crown four years later

Barry Bonds waves to the crowd after he hit a home run in his first at-bat for the Giants in 1993. Bonds won the NL MVP Award that season.

Pleasant Move

The Giants pleased their fans in 2000 by moving from old Candlestick Park to new Pacific Bell Park. The team drew a franchise-record 3.3 million fans that season and finished with 55 home wins to match the New York Mets for the most in the major leagues. Every game in San Francisco that year was a sellout. The new stadium was renamed AT&T Park after the 2003 season.

when Bonds hit 40 home runs. First baseman J. T. Snow and second baseman Jeff Kent combined for 225 RBIs that season. Meanwhile, pitcher Shawn Estes won 19 games and closer Rod Beck saved 37. The eventual champion Florida Marlins swept the Giants in the NLDS. But the 1997 season proved to be the first of eight consecutive winning seasons in San Francisco.

It also proved to be the beginning of one of the greatest scandals in American sports history. By the mid-to-late 1990s, players began hitting previously unheard of numbers of home runs. Bonds was among those players. It was suspected, and then confirmed in later years, that players were using illegal performance-enhancing drugs (PEDs) such as steroids to build strength. However, Bonds has never admitted to knowingly using PEDs to illegally boost his performance.

Whatever the case, Bonds transformed from an excellent power hitter to the greatest slugger in the history of the game. He smashed 49 home runs in 2000 to lead his team to another division championship. Then he set a major league record by slamming 73 home runs in 2001. Every starting player with the 2000 Giants hit 10 or more home runs. But the Giants did not have strong enough pitching to get past the New York Mets in the NLDS.

Frustration reached its height in 2002. The Giants reached the playoffs as the wild-card team. Then they beat the Atlanta Braves and Cardinals to reach the World Series. After five games, the Giants led the Anaheim Angels 3–2 in the World Series. They also led 5–0 in Game 6, but gave up six runs in the seventh and eighth innings to lose the game. Their defeat the next day dashed their hopes for a championship. Giants fans wondered if the team would ever win a title in San Francisco.

Former Giants player Felipe Alou took over as the team's manager in 2003.

But by that time the Giants did not have as much talent as they had in 2002. Bonds was the team's only top batter. They also lacked pitching depth behind 17-game winner Jason Schmidt and closer Tim Worrell. The result was another first-round defeat in the playoffs in 2003.

After the Giants missed the playoffs from 2004 to 2006, Alou was replaced by Bruce Bochy. However, the losing continued. There were highlights for Giants fans, though. On August 7, 2007, Bonds smashed his 756th career home run. That broke the record set by the Hank Aaron 33 years earlier. Bonds, however, was at the end of his career by that time. The 2007 season was the last in his 22-season career.

After four losing seasons, a new nucleus began forming in 2009. The Giants won 88 games

All about Bonds

Barry Bonds was a controversial player toward the end of his career. Many felt he was smug and that his home-run records were tarnished by PEDs. However, his career numbers show why he was one of the most feared batters of all time, even before The Steroid Era. Bonds hit at least 34 home runs every year from 1992 to 2004. He exceeded 100 runs scored and 100 RBIs and led the NL in walks 12 times each. He set an all-time record with 232 walks in 2004. Pitchers that year intentionally walked him 120 times rather than allow him to swing his lethal bat. Bonds was a seven-time MVP.

behind the talented young starting pitchers Tim Lincecum and Matt Cain. Lincecum was especially dominant. He won the NL Cy Young Award in 2008 and 2009 with a combined record of 33–12 and an ERA of 2.55. They continued to shine, along with rookie catcher Buster Posey and closer Brian Wilson, in the World Series season in 2010.

Barry Bonds hits his 714th career home run on May 20, 2006, to tie Babe Ruth for second all time. Bonds retired in 2007 with a record 762 homers.

With a strong core of young players, the Giants are hoping that they don't have to wait nearly as long to bring San Francisco its second World Series title.

TIMELINE

1883	John B. Day and Jim Mutrie form a franchise called the Gothams, who are placed into the NL with Mutrie as manager.
1888	The team, now known as the Giants, wins the first of two consecutive NL titles.
1902	The Giants set the tone for success through the emergence of pitching star Christy Mathewson and by hiring John McGraw as player/manager.
1905	The Giants clinch their first World Series championship with a 2–0 defeat of the Philadelphia Athletics on October 14, a year after refusing to participate in the event due to the supposed inferiority of the AL.
1921	After four consecutive World Series defeats, the Giants secure the 1921 crown on October 13 by defeating the New York Yankees, 1–0, then repeat the accomplishment the next season.
1933	Screwball pitcher Carl Hubbell leads the Giants to another World Series title, which is clinched with a 4–3 win over the Washington Senators on October 7.
1951	The Giants tie the Brooklyn Dodgers for first place in the regular season. They win the pennant on a ninth-inning home run by Bobby Thomson on October 3 in the third and deciding playoff game. The home run becomes known as "The Shot Heard 'Round the World."
1954	Willie Mays and Dusty Rhodes provide the heroics as the Giants sweep the heavily favored Cleveland Indians in the World Series. The Giants end the Series on October 2 with a 7–4 win.

QUOTES AND ANECDOTES

The most famous words ever uttered by former Giants manager Leo Durocher were actually said about the Giants when he was managing the rival Brooklyn Dodgers. But though he is generally credited with saying, "Nice guys finish last," the exact quote was "The nice guys are all over there. In seventh place." Durocher was speaking before a 1946 game against the Giants, who were struggling at the time.

The Giants boasted two no-hitters in 1959, but neither game reached nine innings. Mike McCormick threw a five-inning no-hitter against the Philadelphia Phillies on June 12 and Sam Jones hurled one that lasted seven innings on September 26 against the St. Louis Cardinals. Both games were called due to rain. Games become official once the home team has batted or is ahead in the fifth inning.

Dozens of Giants players are prominent in the team's record books, but no one compares to Willie Mays. Mays is the team's all-time leader in games played (2,857), at-bats (10,477), runs (2,011), hits (3,187), doubles (504), home runs (646), and total bases (5,907). He is second in triples (139), runs batted in (1,859), and third in walks (1,394) and stolen bases (336).

Giants pitcher Stu Miller was blown off the mound by a gust of wind during the 1961 All-Star Game at Candlestick Park. Miller denies it, stating that it merely caused him to sway. But the wind did knock him from his set position on the mound and caused the umpire to call a balk, which moved the runners up and eventually led to the tying run in the ninth inning. The NL still won the game when Willie Mays thrilled his hometown fans by hitting a double and scoring the winning run. Miller was credited with the victory.

GLOSSARY

ace

A team's best starting pitcher.

attendance

The number of fans at a particular game or who come to watch a team play during a particular season.

berth

A place, spot, or position, such as in the baseball playoffs.

closer

A relief pitcher who is called on to pitch, usually in the ninth inning, to protect his team's lead.

contend

To be in the race for a championship or playoff berth.

elite

A player or team that is among the best.

franchise

An entire sports organization, including the players, coaches, and staff.

mediocrity

A state of being average.

momentum

A continued strong performance based on recent success.

pennant

A flag. In baseball, it symbolizes that a team has won its league championship.

postseason

The games in which the best teams play after the regular-season schedule has been completed.

retire

To officially end one's career.

rookie

A first-year player in the major leagues.

wild card

Playoff berths given to the best remaining teams that did not win their respective divisions.

Further Reading

Fost, Dan. *Giants Past & Present.* Osceola, WI: MVP Books, 2010.

Murphy, Brian. *San Francisco Giants: 50 Years.* San Rafael, CA: Insight Editions, 2008.

Vecsey, George. *Baseball: A History of America's Favorite Game.* New York: Modern Library, 2008.

Web Links

To learn more about the San Francisco Giants, visit ABDO Publishing Company online at **www.abdopublishing.com.** Web sites about the Giants are featured on our Book Links page. These links are routinely monitored and updated to provide the most current information available.

Places to Visit

AT&T Park
24 Willie Mays Plaza
San Francisco, CA 94107
415-972-2000
http://mlb.mlb.com/sf/ballpark/index.jsp
This has been the Giants' home field since 2000. Tours are available when the Giants are not playing.

National Baseball Hall of Fame and Museum
25 Main Street
Cooperstown, NY 13326
1-888-HALL-OF-FAME
www.baseballhall.org
This hall of fame and museum highlights the greatest players and moments in the history of baseball. Christy Mathewson, Willie Mays, John McGraw, and Juan Marichal are among the former Giants enshrined there.

Scottsdale Stadium
7408 East Osborn Road
Scottsdale, AZ 85251
480-990-7972
www.scottsdaleaz.gov/stadium/
springtraining.asp
Scottsdale Stadium has been the Giants' spring-training ballpark since 1982.

INDEX

About the Author

Marty Gitlin is a freelance writer based in Cleveland, Ohio. He has written more than 25 educational books, including many about sports. Gitlin has won more than 45 awards during his 25 years as a writer, including first place for general excellence from the Associated Press. He lives with his wife and three children in Ohio.